Animal Alphabet

Funny Edition

Written & Illustrated by

Robert Marsh

This book is dedicated to my 3 beautiful girls who inspired and supported me to create this book.
Thank you Michele, Charlie, & Bella

Written and illustrated by Robert Marsh

Published through Amazon Kindle Direct Publishing

First Edition

A a

A is for Ant

Arty Ant loves to take and store apples
and all other kinds of food.
But not all the ants get to eat, not even
this dude.

Apple
Ant
Avocado

B b

B is for Butterfly

Bella Butterfly loves flapping her beautiful wings in the Spring. She settles on a branch to hear her bird friend Bonnie sing.

Butterfly
Bird
Branch

C c

C is for Cat

Charlie Cat loves to play with her chew
toy in her comfy cat bed.
At night, she sneaks into the kitchen to
take a piece of yummy bread.

Cat
Chew Toy
Comfy Bed

D d

D is for Dog

Debbie Dog loves to bark at the neighbor's cat during the day. At nighttime, she loves to disco dance and play.

Woof!
Dog
Dog Bone
Disco Dance
Music

E e

E is for Elephant

Enzo Elephant is a very playful and fun animal to be around.
He likes playing with his egg and enormous rocks on the ground.

Enormous Rock
Egg
Elephant

F f

F is for Frog

Frankie Frog loves to eat flies relaxing on a lily pad.
He doesn't like sharing his food unless it's with his dad.

Father
Flies
Frog

G g

G is for Giraffe

Geraldine Giraffe has a long neck which makes it easier for her to grab her lunch.
She chews on the grapes, then goes for the branches with a crunch.

Giraffe
Grapes
Grass

H h

H is for Hammerhead

Helen Hammerhead is a happy and friendly shark.
But, for some reason, she has a problem seeing in the dark.

Hair
Happy
Hammerhead

I i

I is for Iguana

Izzy Iguana likes to eat ice cream on his tree.
His favorite flavors are chocolate and cherry.

Ice Cream
Iguana

J j

J is for Jellyfish

Jackie Jellyfish swims around the ocean looking for soap.
She needs to clean her dirty jam-covered jump rope.

SOAP
Jellyfish
Jam-Covered
Jump Rope

Kk

K is for Kangaroo

Kimmie Kangaroo loves to play games and fly her kite.
Kimmie has strong feet, so if anyone tries to take her stuff she can put up a good fight.

Kangaroo
Kite
Kick ball net
Kick ball

L l

L is for Lion

Larry Lion loves to eat lemons in the jungle where he is king.
By the end of the day, his tongue swells up like he was getting a bee sting.

Lion
Lemon

M m

M is for Meerkat

Michele Meerkat likes to eat mushrooms topped with slimy bugs.
Her favorite snack of course are gooey slugs.

Meerkat
Mushroom

Nn

N is for Narwhal

Nathan Narwhal loves to write in his notebook.
When he is swimming too fast, he has to attach it to a hook.

Narwhal
MATH
Notebook

O o

O is for Octopus

Ollie Octopus loves to eat his fruits and veggies during the day.
But, when he eats onions, tears run down his face, and he is unable to see to play.

Onion
Octopus
Orange
Food

P p

P is for Penguin

Peter Penguin likes to jump on his pogo stick.
Today, he learned a new trick.

Penguin
Pogo stick

Q q

Q is for Quail

Quentin Quail loves to sit on the branch bed that his buddy Benny Beaver built. At the end of the day, He likes to relax and rest on his soft quilt.

Quail
Quilt

R r

R is for Rabbit

Robby Rabbit loves playing with his
roller skates down steep hills.
But eating red carrots are what gives
him thrills.

Rabbit
Red Carrot
Roller Skates

S s

S is for Stingray

Stuart Stingray has the biggest smile
from gill to gill.
Especially when he plays with his bestie
Kelli Krill.

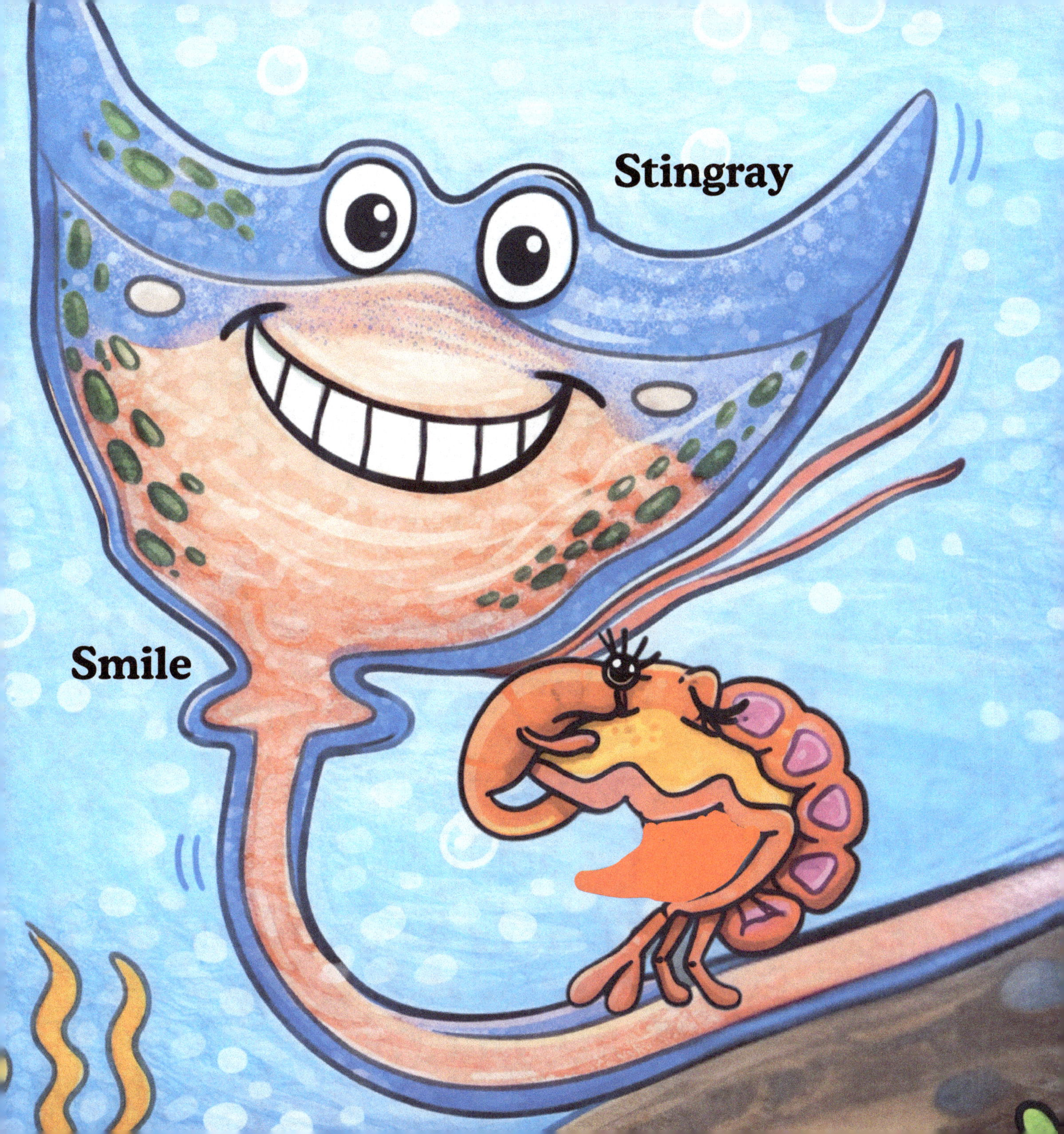

Stingray
Smile

T t

T is for Turtle

Tommy Turtle likes to jump up and down on his new trampoline. Once he figures out how to flip right-side up, he will have a new routine.

Turtle
Tongue
Trampoline

U u

U is for Urchin

Ursula Urchin has spikes all over her body and face.
When she swims to the top of the ocean in the rain, she can't keep her umbrella in place.

Umbrella
Urchin

V v

V is for Viper

Vinny Viper can balance glass objects on his head.
One tiny move and this vase will be on the floor instead.

Vase
Viper

W w

W is for Wolf

Wendy Wolf loves her snacks and
sweets.
Watermelon is her favorite of all her
treats.

Wooooooo
Watermelon
Wolf
Watermelon

X x

X is for X-ray Fish

Xavier X-ray Fish likes to play his tunes. He plays his xylophone most mornings and afternoons.

X-ray Fish
Xylophone

Y y

Y is for Yak

Yoshi Yak loves to play with his yo-yo on his horn.
He's been playing with this toy since he was born.

Yak
Yo-yo

Z z

Z is for Zebra

Zelda Zebra likes to eat zucchini when it is ripe and green.
If anyone tries to take her food, she will get mean.

Zebra
Zucchini

Now you know your ABC's!

What was your favorite animal?

Can you find the Octopus?
How about the Turtle?

How many vegetables can you find?
How many fruits can you find?

Hope you enjoyed learning and laughing
along the way.

www.ingramcontent.com/pod-product-compliance
Lightning Source LLC
Chambersburg PA
CBHW081237130726
47997CB00009B/2904